Arabic Vocabulary Made Easy

Using mnemonics to remember a huge list of Arabic vocabulary (300+ Words)

D.J. WESTERN

ARABIC VOCABULARY MADE EASY

ISBN-10: 0615454526
ISBN-13: 978-0615454528

DEDICATION

To Kathy for keeping me balanced!

ARABIC VOCABULARY MADE EASY

CONTENTS

INTRODUCTION 1

ARABIC MNEMONICS 4

INTERLINGUAL WORD TABOO MNEMONICS 193

WORDS YOU SHOULD ALREADY KNOW 205

INDEX 213

ARABIC VOCABULARY MADE EASY

INTRODUCTION

'Mnemonics' is just a fancy word referring to memory aids. They can be poems, songs, rhymes, or just short catch-phrases used to help you recall something. Basically they can be anything that will help you to remember something else.

In this book there are over 200 mnemonics used to help students of Arabic learn vocabulary terms that are often difficult to associate with anything in the English lexicon. Many of these mnemonics are silly. Some are risqué. Others just provide alternative means of remembering a difficult vocabulary term. The key is that they are intended to help the language learner to remember the real vocabulary word. So if the pronunciation of the mnemonic differs slightly or even greatly from the proper Arabic word, don't worry – the mnemonic is only meant to help you recall the proper term. First try to remember the Arabic vocabulary word on its own. Then you can practice the proper pronunciation of your new vocabulary word.

I've intentionally not grouped the words into categories. As a child you didn't learn to speak by learning lists of words from different classes of vocabulary. Similarly, it won't help you to learn words from a group. Sometimes you'll surprise yourself by finding it easier to learn several words from different groups rather than many terms from one category.

In addition to the 200 mnemonics used in this book, you'll also be introduced to over 100 words that are almost identical to their English counterpart. Obviously there is no need to provide a mnemonic for these terms as you technically already know them.

If at any time you find you don't like the mnemonic presented, try to come up with one on your own. By doing so you'll likely remember the term even more clearly. As a final word, it is my hope that at the end of this book, you'll be motivated to come up with even more mnemonics on your own and thereby be well on your way to a high level of Arabic proficiency. Good luck!

PRONUNCIATION GUIDE

A	ع	Ayn – A very guttural sound made in the back of the throat. Much like the sound "Aaah" while gagging.
d	د	Daal – Same as English letter D
D	ض	Daad – Emphatic. Made like the letter D but with tongue more glued to roof of mouth.
gh	غ	Ghrain – Like a French R in "Rue"
h	ه	Ha – Like the English H
H	ح	H – Sounds like breathing on hands to keep them warm.
kh	خ	Sounds like H, but like you are going to clear your throat.
s	س	Just like English S.
S	ص	Emphatic S. Made like S but with tongue more glued to roof of mouth
t	ت	Like English T
T	ط	Emphatic T. Made like T but with tongue more glued to roof of mouth
th	ذ & ث	Just like "the" and "thought" -- One is fricative, the other is silent.
z	ز	Just like English Z
Z	ظ	Emphatic Z. Made like Z but with tongue more glued to roof of mouth.
'	ء	Like a short "a" but with a pause.

THE ARABIC MNEMONICS

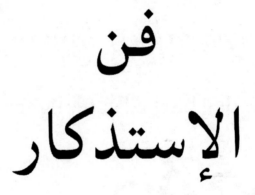

فن

الإستذكار

1. [barq] – Lightning

The dog <u>bar</u>ked at the <u>lightning</u>.

2. [iASaar] – Hurricane

iA Sar a hurricane.

(I saw a hurricane.)

3. [mankhir] – Nostril

What do you usually find in a man's <u>nostril</u>? (Sounds like "<u>man hair</u>")

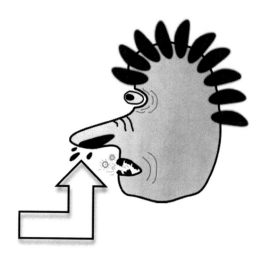

4. [jaar] – Neighbor

I borrowed a <u>jar</u> from my <u>neighbor</u>.

مصدوم

5. [maSdoom] – Shocked

Careful, you might be <u>shocked</u> at the <u>mass</u> of <u>doom</u> you see everywhere!

6. [zíyy] – Costume

Wassup <u>zee</u>? Nice <u>costume</u>!

(Can also be used for uniform.)

7. [tannoora] – Skirt

Look at Noora in that <u>skirt</u>! I have to say that is one really, really <u>tan noora</u>!

8. [Hizaam] – Belt

Remember Shazam? Well the guy with the <u>belt</u> over there...he's our superhero <u>Hizaam</u>!

9. [shaqraa'] – Blonde

Many of you have heard of the singer Shakira. Her <u>blonde</u> hair is enigmatic. When trying to remember the word for <u>blonde</u> just think of her.

كحل

10. [kuHl] – Eyeliner

Ugh. She thinks she is so <u>kuHl</u> (cool) with that <u>eyeliner</u> doesn't she!

11. [washm] – Tattoo

I love my <u>tattoo</u>, but mom said I had to <u>washm</u> off!

12. [bathra] – Blister

Oooh...you have a <u>blister</u>! Go take a <u>bath Ra</u> (Egyptian deity) and take care of it.

13. [síttaara] – Curtain

Hey Alice look behind the <u>curtain</u> and see if you can <u>sittaara</u> (see Tara). "Nope I don't <u>sittaara</u>, just a small door."

14. [saqf] – Ceiling

How do I get my <u>sock off</u> the <u>ceiling</u>
and how in the world did it get there?

15. [sikkeen] – Knife

Cause of death? I sink zat za <u>knife</u> jus <u>sik een</u> 'im (think that the knife just stick in him).

16. *[raff]* – *Shelf*

She keeps that <u>shelf</u> filled to feed all
the riff-<u>raff</u> that visit her shop.

17. [araq] – Insomnia

A soldier in <u>Iraq</u> doesn't get much sleep. It can cause <u>insomnia</u>.

18. [yaduqq] – Knock (verb – lit. he knocks)

Stop <u>knock</u>ing on the door <u>ya duck</u>!

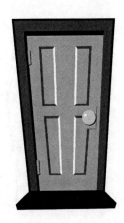

19. [ra's] – Head

Ross has a big head!

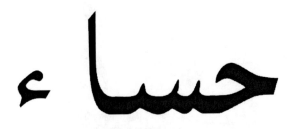

20. [Hisaa'] – Soup

He saw a fly in his soup!

فن

21. [fann] – Art

Art is fun!

22. [takht] – Desk

She <u>taught</u> from behind a <u>desk</u>.

مسطرة

23. [misTara] – Ruler

<u>Miss Tara</u> smacks us with a <u>ruler</u> when we misbehave.

26

وزة

24. [wazza] – Goose

Wazzu(p) goose? What's up goose?

D.J. Western

25. [laqlaaq] – Stork

Some people feel <u>luck luuuck</u> when the <u>stork</u> comes, others don't feel so <u>luck luuucky</u>.

26. *[booSla]* – Compass

You need a <u>compass</u> to take a <u>bus</u> [to] <u>L.A.</u> (busla).

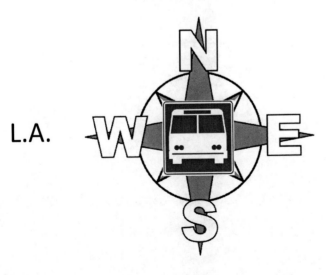

27. [faqadtu] – I lost

I <u>faqadtu</u> (forgot to) remember where my keys were. I guess <u>I lost</u> them.

شقة

28. [shaqqa] – Apartment

She was in <u>shocka</u> 'bout her
<u>apartment</u>.

29. [jidaar] – Wall

Derek <u>Jeter (jidar)</u> is a <u>wall</u> of defense for the New York Yankees.

30. [taj] – Crown

Think about the _Taj Mahal_. It literally means "crown of buildings." Or remember it was built by a king (who wears a crown).

31. [naadir] – Rare

naadir (Nah dear) that dancing deer is not common, it's rare!!

32. *[dabboor] – Wasp*

Bee: "That <u>wasp</u>, he's <u>da bore</u> (boring)! All he does is sting all day...at least I make honey."

He's da bore!

سرطان

33. [saraTaan] – Crab

Did you see any <u>crabs</u> at the beach?
Ya I <u>sar a tahn</u> (saw a ton)!

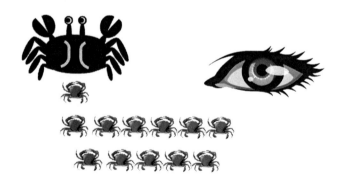

34. [fool] – Bean (Also known as "broad bean.")

Jack was a <u>fool</u> for buying the magic <u>beans</u>.

35. [haykal] – Skeleton

Hi Cal! You're looking a little skinny these days! But I guess for a skeleton that's normal.

مسدس

36. [masadas] – Revolver

To remember this word, think of the
number SIX. A <u>revolver</u> normally has
SIX rounds. In Arabic SIXTH is
"*sadasa.*" "<u>*masadas*</u>" derives from the SIX
rounds in a <u>revolver</u>. Also if the people
at <u>Masada</u> had revolvers, the outcome
might have been different.

37. [filfil] – Pepper

All day long all I do is <u>fill</u>, <u>fill</u>, <u>fill</u>, <u>fill</u>, <u>fill</u>, <u>fill</u> these jars of <u>pepper</u>! Ha Choo!

38. [ghreeb] – Strange

First learn the word "*ghrb*" for "*west*" ... then think what the Arabian Peninsula must have thought of the first people traveling to that area from the west, "boy those people 'from the west' (*ghreeb*) are strange!"

39. [fiTr] – Mushroom

She may act a little crazy, but she's <u>fitter</u> since she started eating <u>mushrooms</u> and stopped eating candy.

40. [DaAm] – Support

A <u>dam</u> gives a great amount of <u>support</u> to a city: water, electricity, fishing, etc.

41. [Karaz] – Cherry

I'm <u>karaz</u>[ee] (crazy) about <u>cherries</u>!

استئناف

42. [Ista'naaf] – Appeal

For Heaven's sake would you give up your constant appeal[s]...it's enough!

43. [feel] – Elephant

Of course I can <u>feel</u> the <u>elephant</u>...he's huge!

44. [faar] – Mouse

The elephant doesn't want to feel the <u>mouse</u>, he wants to get <u>far</u> way from it.

45. [borri] – Acquitted

The pirate was <u>acquitted</u> of stealing the treasure because he <u>buried</u> it and it was never found.

46. [Hoot] – Whale

We all have to give a "<u>hoot</u>" or the <u>whale</u> will go extinct.

Give a "hoot" and save the whale

47. [Toot] – Berry

"toot"ie fruity! I love a nice berry!

48. [dab] – Bear

"Da B[ear]!" Just think of the letters "D" & "B" or the Chicago Bears – "Da Bears." Sounds just like "dub."

Da Bear

"DB"

الفوضى   فضاء   فضة

Silver | Space | Chaos
(fiDDa) | (faDaa') | (al-fawDDa)

49. *Silver Space Chaos*

"Silver, Space, and Chaos" are so similar in Arabic, one way to remember all three is to remember the two letter combination of "fah" and "Dah" and then remember the phrase "Silver Space Chaos is 'fah Dah' (for the) birds."

fiDDA FaDaa' fawDDa!

نقار

50. [naqqaar] – Woodpecker

Woodpecker = Knocker!

خوذة

51. [khootha] – Helmet

I can't tell <u>who the</u> player is under
that <u>helmet</u>.

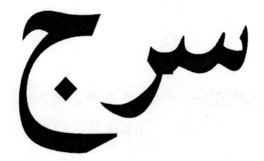

52. [sarj] – Saddle

The officer sat on the <u>sarj</u> (sergeant) because he was acting like a horse.

53. *[sayf] – Sword*

Under the protection of my <u>sword</u>,
you will be <u>safe</u>!

فرار

54. [firaar] – Escape

He's a rich criminal. His <u>escape</u> from prison was in a <u>ferrar</u>[i].

55. [Soof] – Wool

The mystic sect of Muslims known as <u>Sufis</u> get their name from wearing <u>woolen</u> clothing that is uncomfortable. By giving up comfort they remind themselves of their commitment to Allah and their abandonment of earthly things. Think of the <u>Sufi</u> to remember the word for <u>wool</u>.

56. [ibra] – Needle

"Ibra kadibra" said the little fairy whose wand was the size of a needle.

57. [jisr] – Bridge

"Gee sir, that bridge has too many soldiers on it!"

وريد

58. [wareed] – Vein

He was so <u>wareed</u> (worried) that you could see a big <u>vein</u> pop out of his neck.

59. [watar] – String

His guitar <u>string</u>[s] hummed as smooth as running <u>water</u>.

60. [quffaaz] – Glove

The <u>glove</u> <u>quffaaz</u> (covers) her hand.

61. [Habl] – Rope

If you let go of the <u>rope</u> you'd be
lucky to <u>Habl</u> (hobble) away.

62. [madd] – Stretch

You'd have to be <u>madd</u> to <u>stretch</u>
like that!

رقص

63. [raqS] – Dance

She really <u>raqS</u> (rocks) out when
she <u>dances</u>.

64. [farA] – Branch

"Mom, I'm not too <u>far AAAAaaa</u> (scream as he falls off the <u>branch</u>)...out on the <u>branch</u>." Ooops I guess he went too far.

65. [SarSaar] – Cockroach

Aah! I s...s...<u>SarSaar</u> (saw) uh uh <u>cockroach</u>!

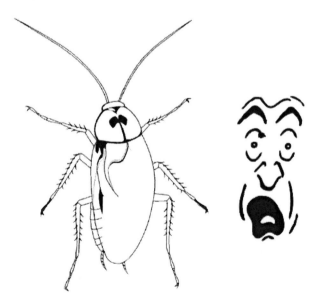

صقر

66. [saqr] – Falcon

The <u>falcon</u> flew around as a mascot at the <u>saqr</u> (soccer) game.

67. [maas] – Diamond

You'll need to a[mass] a lot of money
to afford that diamond.

68. [jumjuma] – Skull

I'm a gonna <u>jumjuma</u> your <u>skull</u>!

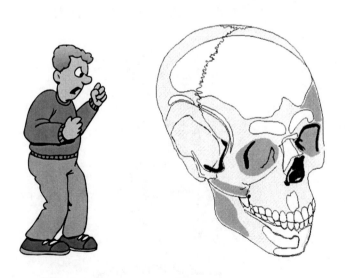

69. [AaZma] – Bone

The skeleton couldn't breath because he had <u>AaZma</u> (asthma).

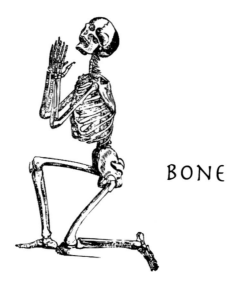

BONE

70. [mukhkh] – Brain

He has cow <u>brains</u> --- <u>mukhkh</u>
(mooo)!

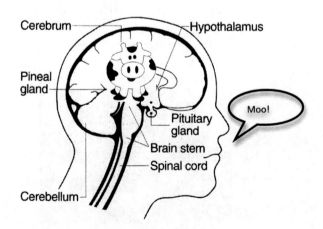

71. [liS] – Thief

When the <u>thief</u> visits you...you usually have <u>liS</u> (less).

72. [Hama] – Father-in-law

My <u>father-in-law</u> is quite a <u>ham[a]</u>!
Or
My <u>father-in-law</u> eats a lot of <u>ham[a]</u>.

73. [Aaboos] – Frown

She <u>frown</u>ed after her car broke down and she had to take <u>Aaboos</u> (a bus) instead.

74. [wishaaH] – Scarf

It's so cold I <u>wish aah H[ad]</u> a <u>scarf</u>.
(aah = I)

منديل

75. [manDeel] –
Handkerchief

What's the <u>deal</u> with that <u>man</u>
(<u>manDeel</u>), he's always blowing his
nose in the same <u>handkerchief</u>. Ick!

76. [HawD] – Sink

HawD (how'd) those sharks get into
the sink?

D.J. Western

77. [duhnee] – Greasy

Duhnee (doesn't he) know how greasy
his hair is?

80

78. [AaTs] – Sneeze

AaTs CHOO!

79. [Aankaboot] – Spider

Ann [got] a boot to smash the spider.

80. [qaws] – Bow

The <u>cows</u> jumped over the rain[<u>bow</u>]s.

81. [lafH] - Sunburn

Sunburn is not a lafHing (laughing) matter...it can cause skin cancer.[*]

___

[*] Usually referred to lafH al-shams (the sun)

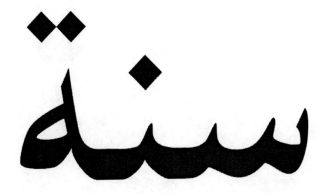

82. [sinna] – Tooth

I'm not a <u>sinna</u> (sinner), I just have a sweet <u>tooth</u>.

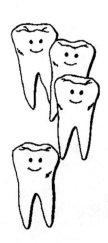

83. [tawatur] – Stress

I need <u>tawatur</u> (to water) my garden to relieve some <u>stress</u>.

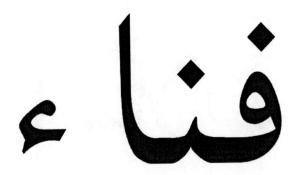

84. [finaa'] – Courtyard

The pool's nice but the <u>courtyard</u> is not <u>finaa'</u>shed [finished] yet.

85. [aslaak] – Wires

Never hire <u>a slaak</u>[er] (slacker) to do your <u>wiring (wires)</u>.
You'll burn your house down.

86. [sulTaaneeya] – Bowl

Put the <u>sultan[eeya]</u>s (sultanas are another name for raisins) in the fruit <u>bowl</u> please.

87. [milʕAaqa] – Spoon

Eat your cereal with <u>milAaqa</u> (milk) and a <u>spoon</u>.

مخدة

88. [mikhadda] – Pillow

Can't you hit <u>mikhadda</u> (me harder) than that?

89. [mismaar] – Nail

With these <u>nail</u>[s] you'll never <u>mismaar</u>
(miss the mark).

90. [Sadma] – Shock

Don't be <u>Sadma</u>, he's in <u>shock</u> but he'll be all right.

D.J. Western

91. [khalaaT] – Blender

You can put <u>khalaaT</u> (a lot) in that <u>blender</u>.

92. [mushtashaar] – Consultant

Listen here son, every expert consultant will tell you, mushtashaar (mustaches are) bad.

93. [janeen] – Embryo

Congratulations! Do you see the embryo on the monitor? What will you name your baby? Janeen.

94. [wazn] – Weight

That <u>wazn</u> (wasn't) very heavy.

95. [shurfa] – Balcony

You'll <u>shurfa[ll]</u> (sure fall) if you lean
too far off the <u>balcony</u>.

مصعد

96. [miSAad] – Elevator

"mi SAad (me sad)!" "We'll then take the elevator, it will 'lift' your spirits.

99

D.J. Western

أَرِيكة

97. [areeka] – Sofa

Areeka! (Eureka) I found you!
Hiding in the sofa!

100

98. [shawka] – Fork

I <u>shawka</u>[ld] (sure could) use a <u>fork</u> to eat this.

99. [furn] – Oven

My <u>oven</u> is really more like a <u>furn</u>[ace].

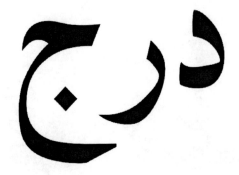

100. [durj] – Drawer

Durj [there is] a lot of stuff in dat drawer.

101. [fuwaT] – Towels

This is <u>fuwaT</u> (for what)? <u>Towels</u> are
for drying yourself off, silly!

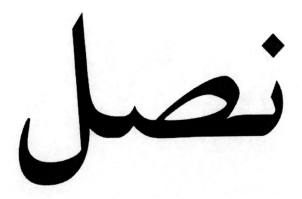

102. [naSl] – Blade

A good way to unclog the <u>naSl</u> (nozzle) is to take a <u>blade</u> and pick away the gunk.

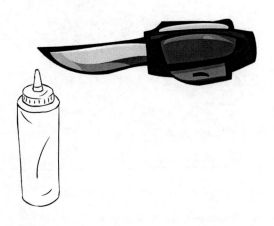

103. [milaa'a] – Sheet

Now I <u>milaa'a</u> down to sleep I pray
the bed to have a <u>sheet</u>.

104. [khashab] – Wood

Khashab (hush up) or I'll knock you
over the head with this piece of wood.

105. [minshaar] – Saw

Min shaar (men sure) like to saw things.

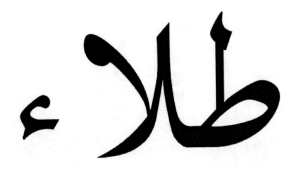

106. [Tilaa] – Paint

a[Tilaa] (Atilla) the Hun retired from killing and now he just paint[s] everywhere he goes.

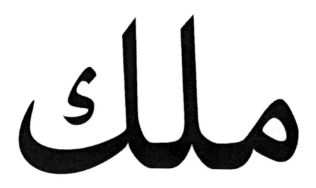

107. [malak] – King

The verb "<u>malak</u>" in Arabic means "to own" -- The key to remembering this word is to remember that the <u>king</u> basically owns you.

108. [waHsh] – Monster

<u>WaHsh</u> your face, you look like a <u>monster</u>.

109. [sayyaara] – Car

Many <u>cars</u> are named "<u>sierra</u>" – think of them: Ford Sierra; GMC Sierra; Suzuki Sierra.

110. [baariz] – Prominent

He is a <u>prominent</u> figure from <u>baaris</u> (Paris).

111. [maSdam] – Bumper

When I drive a <u>bumper</u> car I always hit my target and never seem to <u>maSdam</u> (miss them) with my <u>bumper</u>.

112. [mutumayez] –

Distinct

I think George and May, our cows, are in love. George's <u>moo to may ez</u> much more <u>distinct</u> than his moo to any other cow.

113. [riwaaq] – Porch

Ree waaq (we walk) out onto the porch to say "hi" to our neighbors.

114. [qufl] – Lock

Qufl (careful) when you exit, the lock
is automatic and you may end up
locked out.

115. [khizaana] – Closet

"<u>khizaana</u>, <u>khizaana</u> (hosanna, hosanna), in the highest..." What I sing when my <u>closet</u> is clean!

116. [turba] – Soil

Careful not to drop your <u>turba</u>[n] in the <u>soil</u> or it will get dirty.

117. [soor] – Fence

I'm <u>soor</u> (sore), do I have to keep painting the <u>fence</u>?

118. [najeel] – Grass

Najeel (Nigel) likes to walk barefoot
on the grass.

119. [aasif] – I'm sorry

120. [qawee] – Strong

Think of a <u>strong</u> Aussie: "<u>Cooooe</u> Cobber!"

121. [balad] – Country

It's a Country Western <u>ballad</u> about my home <u>country</u>.

122. [sharq] – East

Sharq[s] (sharks) always prefer to eat from the east.

123. [qarn] – Century

It's the qarn[ival] of the century!

124. [waqt] – Time

I <u>waqt</u> (walked) to work in no <u>time</u> at all.

125. [attaqweem] – Calendar

The <u>attaqweem</u>[ade] (the attack we made) took a whole <u>calendar</u> year.

ضاحية

126. [DaaHaya] – Suburb

<u>DaaHaya</u> (the higher) up on the ladder of success you go, the better the <u>suburb</u> you live in.

رأس كتف ركبة قدم

أنف عين أذن فم

127. [ra's, kitif, ruqba, qadam, anf, Aayn, udhun, fam] – Head, Shoulder, Knee, Foot, Nose, Eye, Ear, Mouth.

Sing to tune of "head, shoulders, knees, and toes." i.e. ra's ki tif ruq ba qa dam ruq ba qa dam ruq ba qa dam ra's ki tif ruq ba qa dam anf Aayn udhun and fam!

Literally: head, shoulder, knee, foot, knee, foot, knee, foot, head, shoulder, knee, foot, nose, eye, ear, mouth!

درس	dars	Lesson	Core tri-lateral root
ادرس	adroos	I study	I'm doing the verb. Literally, "I'm lessoning = studying"
ادرّس	oodarris	I teach	I'm doing the verb to others "making others learn lesson = teach"
مدرسة	madrasa	School	Place of lesson

128. [dars] – Lesson

Lesson for the day: Trilateral roots.
"I dars say 'dal' 'rah' 'seen' is da easiest
trilateral root in Arabic!"

*Learn the trilateral root for your
vocabulary word and then the world
opens up with new word possibilities.*

129. [joora] - Manhole

The joora (juror) fell down a manhole. Too bad it wasn't the lawyers on the case instead!

130. [laafita] – Street Sign

Laafita[p] (laugh it up) but we just missed the <u>sign</u> and now we are lost.

131. [jithr] – Root

The <u>root</u>[s] of the tree <u>jithr</u> (gather) where the water is.

132. [booma] – Owl

The mouse looked up and <u>BOOMA</u>!
He was gone. The <u>owl</u> snatched him
up before he could flee.

133. [al-marreekh] – Mars

<u>Al marreekh</u> (I'll marry) a man from <u>Mars</u> sooner than I'd marry you!

حمامة

134. [Hamaama] – Pigeon

Remember that the word for "bathroom" in Arabic is "Hammaam." Now just remember that all <u>pigeons</u> do is poop everywhere. Their world is their bathroom – ergo... "<u>Hamaama</u>"

135. [qamr] - Moon

The Comoros is a small island country north of Madagascar. Its name comes from "qamr" or moon in Arabic. If you will recall the crescent is a symbol of Islam. The moon, when not full, often makes a crescent. Thus the Comoros is a reference to the crescent moon or Islam.

THINK Comoros

138

136. [maTar] – Rain

My <u>maTar</u> (mother) won't let us play in the <u>rain</u>.

137. [kawkab] – Planet

Sorry, there is no such thing as a
kawkab (cow cab) on planet earth, but
I hear the planet mars has cow cycles.

غابة

138. [ghaaba] – Forest

The ghaaba (robba *like robber*) hid in the forest. He called himself ghaaba hood.

إطلاق

139. [ITlaaq] – Launch

Help! I can't stop the <u>launch</u>, the system...<u>it laaq</u>[ed] up (it locked up)! We are go in 10, 9, 8, 7...

140. [al-mustanqaA] –

Swamp

The swamp almost stank Aaah (al-mustanqaA). Wait...never mind, it does really stink.

141. [madaar] – Orbit

He gets <u>madaar</u> (madder) and <u>madaar</u> and <u>madaar</u> until he goes into <u>orbit</u>!

صحراء

142. [SaHraa'] – Desert

Sahara desert.

143. [raml] – Sand

The <u>ram'll</u> (ram will) slip in the <u>sand</u>.

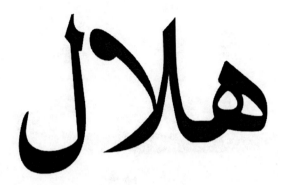

144. *[hilaal] – Crescent moon*

"Hilal" is the term used in Islam to mean that it is permissible to eat (or otherwise engage with). It is like "kosher" in Judaisim. The symbol of the crescent moon refers to Islam. Once you remember this symbol, it is easy to remember the word "hilal" for crescent moon. When shopping in Arab food stores, you will see the word "hilal" on products indicating they are permissible - or under the crescent moon.

147

145. [khayT] – Thread

I <u>khayT</u> (hate) <u>thread</u>ing a needle.

146. [al-jazeera] –Island

The news organization "Al Jazeera" is based out of Doha, Qatar which is on the Arabian peninsula. It literally means "the island" as a reference to the Arabian peninsula. Think of that news organization to remember the word "island."

147. [furshaah] – Brush

Remember *The Brady Bunch*, "Marsha, Marsha, Marsha..." Marsha was always brushing her hair. Now just think "furshaah, furshaah, furshaah" and picture an Arab Marsha named "Furshaah."

صدف

148. *[Sadaf] – Sea Shell*

Pick another <u>sea shell</u>, that one looks like part of it has been <u>Sadaf</u> (sawed off).

149. [naadee] – Club

Don't go to that <u>club</u>, it is very <u>naadee</u> (naughty).

150. [aghranee] – I sing

The rock band *Flock of Seagulls* <u>sings</u>, "I ran (so far away)."

<u>Sing "aghran[ee]"</u> to that tune. "And <u>aghran[ee]</u>, <u>aghran[ee]</u> so far away...couldn't get away..."

153

D.J. Western

151. [aalaat] – Instruments

There are <u>aalaat</u> (a lot) of <u>instruments</u> in a band or orchestra.

كمان

152. [kamaan] – Violin

Kamaan (come on) sweetheart
practice your violin!

153. [hadaf] – Target (goal)

Did you take out 'target F'? No Sir, I hadaf (had F) in my sights, but I missed.

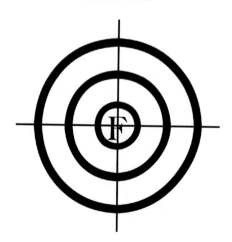

154. [sinaara] – Fishing Pole

I am not a <u>sinaara</u> (sinner), I just like to fish. Ah, but you are a <u>sinaara</u> because you spent $100,000 on a <u>fishing pole</u>!

155. [HiSaan] – Horse

John Wayne is not here. <u>HiSaan</u> (he's on) a <u>horse</u>.

156. [thahab] – Gold

The hab[s] (the haves) hab <u>gold</u> and
the hab nots don't.

157. [sibaaq] – Race

See Bock run. Run Bock run. It is a race.

158. [Hadeed] – Iron

Ha deed (her deed) for the day was to iron clothes.*

---

* Note the word "Hadeed" refers to the mineral and not the device used on clothing (mikwaah). This is just a mnemonic to help you remember the word for the mineral.

فريق

159. [fareeq] – Team

That <u>team</u> is filled with a bunch of <u>fareeq</u>[s] (freaks). They're huge!

بضائع

160. [baDaa'iA] – Cargo

The reason we all are fat and have a baDaa'iA (bad diet) is because we only get <u>cargo</u> from Candyland.

161. [winsh] – Crane

Someone needs to help that <u>winsh</u> (wench) get down from that <u>crane</u>!

162. [meenaa'] – Port/Harbor

Don't go to that <u>port</u>, the pirates are <u>meenaa'</u> (meaner) there than here.

D.J. Western

تأشيرة

163. [tasheera] – Visa

In New Zealand, you need a <u>visa</u>
<u>tasheera</u> (to sheer a) sheep.

164. [Tayyaar] – Pilot

The <u>pilot</u>'s call sign is "<u>tayyaar</u>" (tire) because he blows them on landing.

165. *[farmala]* – Act of Braking

<u>Brake</u> or you'll hit the <u>farm ala</u> (Oliver – 'ala' for short)!

166. [miqbaD] – Handle

<u>MicbaD</u>! Bad Mic! Let go of the <u>handle</u>! It is time to get off the bus.

169

167. [amtíAa] – Luggage

The luggage is amtiAa
(empty...Aaah)! We've been robbed.

خريطة

168. [khareeTa] – Map

khareeTa[p] (hurry it up) and get a map or ask for directions!

169. [naHt] – Sculpture

The <u>sculpture</u> is <u>naHt</u> (not) very good.

170. [Tabeeb] – Doctor

Tabeeb or not Tabeeb that is the question. Whether it is time to go to the doctor.

مبيد آفات

171. [mubeed aafaat] – Pesticide

Drink <u>pesticide</u> and you'll be <u>mubeed aafaat</u> (morbid and fat).

172. [maHSool] - Crop

I put <u>maHSool</u> (my soul) into that <u>crop</u>! I hope it survives.

173. [daleel] – Evidence

There's just <u>daleel</u> (a little) bit of <u>evidence</u> against me. I don't think I'll be found guilty.

174. [milaf] – File

Don't make <u>milaf</u> (me laugh) your <u>file</u>
is filled with arrest warrants. I can't
hire you!

شاشة

175. [shaasha] – Screen

Shaasha[p]! The movie is about to start.

176. [dabbaasa] – Stapler

Dabbaasa (the boss) took my stapler.
I need dabbaasa to know that the
stapler is mine.

177. [aadaab] – Literature

aadaab[le] (a dabble) into literature
makes anyone smart.

178. [ghabee] – Stupid

Ghabee (Robbie) is stupid.

Robbie

179. [taSdeer] – Export

Canadian <u>export</u>? What do they do just <u>taSdeer</u> (toss deer) from their backyard into the United States?

EXPORT

180. [asad] – Lion

Bashar Al-<u>Asad</u> is the President of Syria. His family name means "the <u>Lion</u>." Although he was an ophthalmologist by trade before becoming President, his family is as strong in Syria as a den of <u>lions</u>. Think of him as a <u>lion</u> to remember the term, "<u>asad</u>."

181. [Hisaab] – Bill

Hisaab[ed] (he sobbed) at the bill. It was too high!

182. [lawz] – Almond

These <u>almonds</u> are <u>lawz</u>[y] (lousy)!

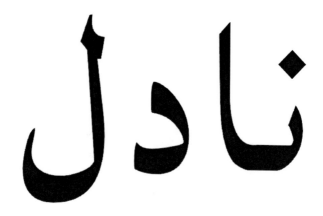

183. *[naadil] – Waiter*

If you <u>naadil</u> (nod he'll) come to serve you. Who? The <u>waiter</u> of course.

184. [baqsheesh] – Tip

He's not coming baq....sheesh! (back...sheesh)
No tip for him.

Or

One baq (buck)? Sheesh! What a terrible tip!

185. [zayt] – Oil (food)

<u>Zay ate</u> ('they ate' with a French accent shortened into one word) the bread with olive <u>oil</u>.

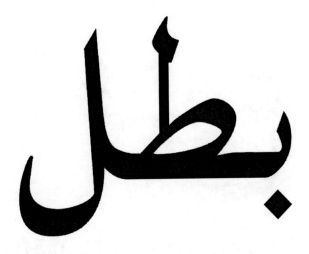

186. [baTal] – Hero

Heroes are forged in baTal (battle).

187. [naAnaaA] – Mint

My <u>naAnaaA</u> (Nana) loves <u>mint</u>.
That's why we call my <u>naAnaaA</u>,
"Nana <u>minty</u>."

188. [qirfa] – Cinnamon

Cinnamon is the qirfa (cure for) most diseases.

189. [thoom] – Garlic

I [a]<u>thoom</u>[ed] (assumed) you liked <u>garlic</u> because you smell so bad.

Interlingual Word Taboos

ENTER WITH CAUTION

One of the easiest ways to remember new vocabulary in any foreign language is to find interlingual word taboos. Because cursing in one's native tongue creates an emotional response for the speaker, hearing that same sound in a foreign tongue creates a similar response (even though you are not saying anything wrong in the foreign tongue). It is therefore often difficult for a person speaking in a foreign language to say a vocabulary word if it is also a forbidden word in your own language. One benefit of this, however, is that the interlingual word taboo is easier to remember. The following words are examples of interlingual word taboos. WARNING: ENTER WITH CAUTION!

190. [shitaa'] – Winter

Winter is the <u>shitaa'</u>[ist] (shitiest) season. It is too cold!

مرقاق

191. [mirqaq] – Rolling pin

That's not a <u>mirqaq</u> (mere cock), that's a <u>rolling pin</u>!

192. [dam] – Blood

What you say when you cut yourself and see <u>blood</u>, "Oh <u>dam</u> (damn)!"

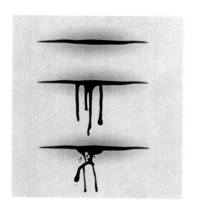

193. [mifakk] –
Screwdriver

Fakk...Screw, "fakk mi" "mifakk"....screwdriver. Self-explanatory.

194. [Huboob] – Bean

Huboob[s] (her boobs) were shaped
like pinto beans.

195. [Hareer] – Silk

Hareer (her rear) was covered with silk panties.

Silk

196. [fakk] – Jaw

What you might say if someone slaps
you in the jaw, "ah fakk!"

197. [HayD] –

Menstruation

I <u>HayD</u> (hate) that time of the month.

198. [sutra] – Jacket

It's hard to do kama <u>sutra</u> when wearing a <u>jacket</u>!

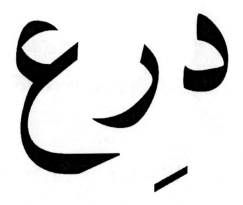

199. [dirA] – Slip

dirA (dear uh) that <u>slip</u> looks very sexy.*

---

* *dirA* literally means "shield." As a slip it shields a woman's body from transparency under a dress.

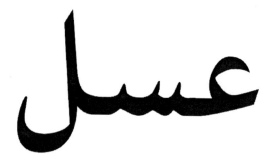

200. [Asal] – Honey

That <u>Asal</u> (asshole) tried to take my <u>honey</u>.

Words You Likely Already Know!

These 100+ words should be easy to learn as they are pretty much the same in Arabic as in English

Words you should already know

1.	هرمون	hormoon	Hormone
2.	شورت	short	Shorts
3.	تي شيرت	tee shirt	T-Shirt
4.	ميل	meel	Mile
5.	متر	metr	meter
6.	صندل	Sandal	Sandle
7.	طن	Tunn	Ton
8.	جينز	jeenz	Jeans
9.	جرام	graam	Gram
10.	روب	roob	Gown
11.	ليموزين	lemoozeen	Limousine
12.	سويت شيرت	sweet shirt	Sweatshirt
13.	ديزل	deezil	Diesel
14.	جاكيت	jaakayt	Jacket
15.	جراج	garaaj	Garage
16.	بلوزة	bilooza	Blouse
17.	جيل	gel	Gel
18.	بولو	bolo	Polo
19.	ورنيش	warneesh	Varnish
20.	كبل	kabl	Cable
21.	شامبو	shaambu	Shampoo
22.	بيجاما	beejaamaa	Pajama
23.	ميكروويف	meekroweef	Microwave
24.	يوجا	yogaa	Yoga

More words you should already know

25.	قثطرة	qathTara	Catheter
26.	مسكرة	maskara	Mascara
27.	مراة	mir'aa	Mirror
28.	ترمومتر	termommetr	Thermometer
29.	بودرة	bowdra	Powder
30.	قطن	qatan	Cotton
31.	فيروس	feyroos	Virus
32.	الهملايا	al-himalayaa	Himalayas
33.	سيبيريا	seebeereeaa	Siberia
34.	مللیمتر	mileemetr	Millimeter
35.	كولاج	kolaaj	Collage
36.	ياردة	yarda	Yard
37.	باينت	baynt	Pint
38.	لتر	litr	Liter
39.	بستيل	basteel	Pastel
40.	نيلون	naylon	Nylon
41.	رادار	raadaar	Radar
42.	جالون	gaaloon	Gallon
43.	تلسكوب	teleskob	Telescope
44.	كرتونة	kartoona	Carton
45.	سينما	seenimaa	Cinema
46.	سمندار	samandaar	Salamander
47.	اورانوس	uraanoos	Uranus
48.	نبتون	nebtoon	Neptune

More words you should already know

49.	فلم	*film*	Film
50.	إخطبوس	*akhTobus*	Octopus
51.	بلوتو	*bluto*	Pluto
52.	كهف	*kahf*	Cave
53.	جرانيت	*graaneet*	Granite
54.	ككاتوة	*kakaatooa*	Cockatoo
55.	أوبال	*aobaal*	Opal
56.	توباز	*tobaaz*	Topaz
57.	إجوانة	*Igwana*	Iguana
58.	جمل	*jamal*	Camel
59.	زرافة	*zeraafa*	Giraffe
60.	راكون	*raakoon*	Raccoon
61.	كنغر	*kanghar*	Kangaroo
62.	نيكل	*neekel*	Nickel
63.	أمثست	*amathest*	Amethyst
64.	زنك	*zink*	Zinc
65.	بوليّاستير	*boleeyesteer*	Polyester
66.	جرافيت	*graafeet*	Graphite
67.	كوارتز	*kwaartz*	Quartz
68.	أص	*aS*	Ace
69.	جوكر	*joker*	Joker
70.	بوكر	*boker*	Poker
71.	كلارينيت	*klareeneet*	Clarinet
72.	باصون	*baaSoon*	Bassoon

More words you should already know

73.	بريدج	breedj	Bridge
74.	دومينو	domeeno	Dominoes
75.	فلوت	flut	Flute
76.	إوبو	aobo	Oboe
77.	راديو	raadeeo	Radio
78.	ستريو	stereeoo	Stereo
79.	بيكيني	beekeenee	Bikini
80.	جاز	jaaz	Jazz
81.	بلوز	blooz	Blues
82.	بيكولو	beekooloo	Piccolo
83.	توبا	toobaa	Tuba
84.	يخت	yakht	Yacht
85.	سوناتة	sonaata	Sonata
86.	فيولا	feeoolaa	Viola
87.	تشيللو	tchelloo	Cello
88.	روديو	rodeeo	Rodeo
89.	باياردو	bayeeardo	Pool
90.	سنوكر	snookr	Snooker
91.	جمنازيوم	jimnaazeeyoom	Gym
92.	باليه	baaleeh	Ballet
93.	فودكا	fadkaa	Vodka
94.	بيرة	beera	Beer
95.	شوكولاتة	shawkolata	Chocolate
96.	كولا	kola	Cola

More words you should already know

97.	بيانو	*beaano*	Piano
98.	بيتزا	*beetza*	Pizza
99.	فاكس	*faaks*	Fax
100.	بار	*baar*	Bar
101.	ميكروفون	*meekrofon*	Microphone
102.	ليمون	*leemoon*	Lemon
103.	ساونا	*saaoonaa*	Sauna
104.	موسيقى	*museeka*	Music

Many French words are found in Arabic too

Here are some examples:

105.	بنطلون	*banTalon*	Pantalon (Pants)
106.	قميص	*qameeS*	Chemise (Shirt)
107.	دش	*doosh*	Douche (Shower)
108.	موضة	*mooda*	Mode (Fashion)

Also most country names are almost the same in Arabic

Here are some examples:

109.	كندا	*kanadaa*	Canada
110.	جرينلند	*greenland*	Greenland
111.	هايتي	*haytee*	Haiti
112.	بيرو	*beyru*	Peru
113.	برازيل	*braazeel*	Brazil
114.	زامبيا	*zaambeea*	Zambia
115.	مالي	*maalee*	Mali

CPSIA information can be obtained at www.ICGtesting.com
Printed in the USA
LVOW031952270312

275005LV00011B/82/P